This Book Belongs to:

*There is power in writing
things down.
Motivational counselors say,
'Write it down, and make a plan.'
I say, 'Write it down,
so you don't forget,
and it may manifest!"*
– June A Ramsay

Write It Down.

So, You Remember.

Write It Down.

So, You Remember.

Write It Down.

So, You Remember.

Write It Down.

So, You Remember.

Write It Down.

So, You Remember.

Write It Down.

So, You Remember.

Write It Down.

So, You Remember.

Write It Down.

So, You Remember.

Write It Down.

So, You Remember.

Write It Down.

So, You Remember.

Write It Down.

So, You Remember.

Write It Down.

So, You Remember.

Write It Down.

So, You Remember.

Write It Down.

So, You Remember.

Write It Down.

So, You Remember.

Write It Down.

So, You Remember.

Write It Down.

So, You Remember.

Write It Down.

So, You Remember.

Write It Down.

So, You Remember.

Write It Down.

So, You Remember.

Write It Down.

So, You Remember.

Write It Down.

So, You Remember.

Write It Down.

So, You Remember.

Write It Down.

So, You Remember.

Write It Down.

So, You Remember.

Write It Down.

So, You Remember.

Write It Down.

So, You Remember.

Write It Down.

So, You Remember.

Write It Down.

So, You Remember.

Write It Down.

So, You Remember.

Write It Down.

So, You Remember.

Write It Down.

So, You Remember.

Write It Down.

So, You Remember.

Write It Down.

So, You Remember.

Write It Down.

So, You Remember.

Write It Down.

So, You Remember.

Write It Down.

So, You Remember.

Write It Down.

So, You Remember.

Write It Down.

So, You Remember.

Write It Down.

So, You Remember.

Write It Down.

So, You Remember.

Write It Down.

So, You Remember.

Write It Down.

So, You Remember.

Write It Down.

So, You Remember.

Write It Down.

So, You Remember.

Write It Down.

So, You Remember.

Write It Down.

So, You Remember.

Write It Down.

So, You Remember.

Write It Down.

So, You Remember.

Write It Down.

So, You Remember.

Write It Down.

So, You Remember.

Write It Down.

So, You Remember.

Write It Down.

So, You Remember.

Write It Down.

So, You Remember.

Write It Down.

So, You Remember.

Write It Down.

So, You Remember.

Write It Down.

So, You Remember.

Write It Down.

So, You Remember.

Write It Down.

So, You Remember.

Write It Down.

So, You Remember.

Write It Down.

So, You Remember.

Write It Down.

So, You Remember.

Write It Down.

So, You Remember.

Write It Down.

So, You Remember.

Write It Down.

So, You Remember.

Write It Down.

So, You Remember.

Write It Down.

So, You Remember.

Write It Down.

So, You Remember.

Write It Down.

So, You Remember.

Write It Down.

So, You Remember.

Write It Down.

_____

_____

_____

_____

_____

_____

_____

_____

_____

_____

_____

So, You Remember.

Write It Down.

So, You Remember.

Write It Down.

So, You Remember.

Write It Down.

So, You Remember.

Write It Down.

So, You Remember.

Write It Down.

So, You Remember.

Write It Down.

So, You Remember.

Write It Down.

So, You Remember.

Write It Down.

So, You Remember.

Write It Down.

So, You Remember.

Write It Down.

So, You Remember.

Write It Down.

So, You Remember.

Write It Down.

So, You Remember.

Write It Down.

So, You Remember.

Write It Down.

So, You Remember.

Write It Down.

So, You Remember.

Write It Down.

So, You Remember.

Write It Down.

So, You Remember.

Write It Down.

So, You Remember.

Write It Down.

So, You Remember.

Write It Down.

So, You Remember.

Write It Down.

So, You Remember.

Write It Down.

So, You Remember.

Write It Down.

So, You Remember.

Write It Down.

So, You Remember.

Write It Down.

So, You Remember.

Write It Down.

So, You Remember.

Write It Down.

So, You Remember.

Write It Down.

So, You Remember.

Write It Down.

So, You Remember.

Write It Down.

So, You Remember.

Write It Down.

So, You Remember.

Write It Down.

So, You Remember.

Write It Down.

So, You Remember.

Write It Down.

So, You Remember.

Write It Down.

So, You Remember.

Write It Down.

So, You Remember.

Write It Down.

So, You Remember.

Write It Down.

____

____

____

____

____

____

____

____

____

____

So, You Remember.

Write It Down.

So, You Remember.

Write It Down.

So, You Remember.

Write It Down.

So, You Remember.

Write It Down.

So, You Remember.

Write It Down.

So, You Remember.

Write It Down.

So, You Remember.

Write It Down.

So, You Remember.

Write It Down.

So, You Remember.

Write It Down.

So, You Remember.

Write It Down.

So, You Remember.

Write It Down.

So, You Remember.

Write It Down.

So, You Remember.

Write It Down.

So, You Remember.

Write It Down.

So, You Remember.

Write It Down.

So, You Remember.

Write It Down.

So, You Remember.

Write It Down.

So, You Remember.

Write It Down.

So, You Remember.